Let's see... About Me and My Family

A WORKBOOK OF FUN WAYS TO THINK AND LEARN ABOUT YOUR FAMILY

by Beth Ann Marcozzi & Hennie M. Shore
Illustrated by Steve Barr

The Center for Applied Psychology, Inc.
King of Prussia, Pennsylvania

LET'S SEE. . . ABOUT ME AND MY FAMILY
A Workbook of Fun Ways to Think and Learn About Your Family
by Beth Ann Marcozzi & Hennie M. Shore
Illustrated by Steve Barr

Published by:
The Center for Applied Psychology, Inc.
P.O. Box 61587, King of Prussia, PA 19406 U.S.A.
Tel. 1-800-962-1141

The Center for Applied Psychology, Inc. is the publisher of Childswork/Childsplay, a catalog of products for mental health professionals, teachers, and parents who wish to help children with their social and emotional growth.

ISBN 1-882732-44-8

CONTENTS

INTRODUCTION

Let's See. . . About Me and My Family is a workbook of exercises designed to help children learn about their relationships with the people in their families. The book is divided into four sections: relationships within the family, family values, problems that affect the family, and future issues.

The first section deals with feelings, attitudes, and the unique connections family members have with one another. The second section presents activities that provoke children to think about what's really important when it comes to family values and norms. The third section challenges children to delve into many different kinds of problems families face as a unit, and the fourth section presents a fun forum in which children can envision themselves as adults and decide how they would like their own children to behave.

Using this book. . .

This workbook was primarily intended for use by counselors and teachers to help individuals or groups of children learn about themselves within the context of their families. Each activity is designed to give children new ways to think about how their family functions as a unit, and to reinforce this information by writing and drawing. The exercises can also be read by an adult to groups of children and then used as the basis for discussion.

SECTION I: RELATIONSHIPS IN THE FAMILY

1. FAMILY FEELINGS

Have you ever seen a family having fun together as a unit? Maybe it was at the park, or in a restaurant. You may have thought, "Look at them. They're so lucky to be able to have fun together." But the reality is that all families have problems and conflicts on some level. Understanding these conflicts and allowing everyone the opportunity to express their feelings to fellow family members is as important to the functioning of a family as having a place to live or food to eat.

Everyone has different feelings at different times. Sometimes you can tell how a person is feeling by the expression on his face or from his actions. Desiree's father comes home from work looking serious and worried. Desiree thinks, "It seems like Dad had a bad day at work. Instead of asking him for help with my homework, maybe I should ask someone else."

Why do you think Desiree thought it would be better not to bother her father?

_____

_____

_____

What do you think her father would have said if she had decided to ask for his help?

_____

_____

_____

How do you think her father would have felt if he had known that she was being considerate of his feelings?

_____

_____

_____

When Samantha got home from school, she saw her mother sitting at the kitchen table with a sad look and her hand over her face. She knew something was wrong. She gave her mom a hug and asked if she was okay. Her mother gave her a big hug back, smiled, and told Samantha that she just wasn't feeling very well. Even though she knew something was wrong, Samantha left her mother alone to rest and went to do her homework.

How do you think Samantha could tell something was wrong?

_____

_____

_____

Do you think Samantha's mom should have told her what was really wrong?
Why or why not?

_____

_____

_____

Do you think Samantha should have forced her mom to tell her what was wrong?
Why or why not?

_____

_____

_____

Describe a situation where you could tell by the facial expressions and actions of a family member how he or she was feeling, and what you did to show him or her that you understood.

_____

_____

_____

2. I HAVE FEELINGS, TOO

Just as others want you to understand their feelings, you would like them to understand yours. But sometimes, when you're very angry, it's hard for them to understand how you really feel, behind all that anger. Throwing a tantrum, yelling at your mother, or taking it out on your brother or sister won't help them to understand your feelings.

Michael studied very hard for his science test and thought he did well enough to get an "A." But he got a "C," and he was furious! When his little brother Paul ran up to greet him after school, Michael was still so mad that he pushed Paul down on the ground and Paul began to cry.

Do you think this was a good way for Michael to express his anger and to let his family know he was upset?

_____

_____

_____

What could Michael have done instead of pushing his brother?

_____

_____

_____

What are some appropriate ways to help your family understand that you are really upset?

_____

_____

_____

Sarah was proud of her artwork, but her parents thought she should spend her free time playing outside with the other kids instead of drawing in her room all the time. Every time she would show them her drawings, they would say, "That's nice, but why don't you go outside and play?"

Why do you think Sarah's parents wanted her to play with the other kids?

_____

_____

_____

Why was Sarah upset about her parents not caring about her artwork?

_____

_____

_____

What could Sarah do to make her parents see that her work was important to her?

_____

_____

_____

Draw yourself doing an activity that you love to do.

3. WHEN THINGS DON'T GO AS PLANNED

Sometimes you plan for something, and you think you know how things will go, but then something happens, and things don't go as planned. Often, someone in your family can be the cause of it. That's why it's good to be able to "go with the flow," and not be disappointed when things don't work out. Life is full of disappointments, and learning to live with and accept them makes you stronger in the long run.

Hallie had been looking forward to going to the movies with her family all week, but as the family prepared to go, she began to feel sick. She thought, "I won't tell anyone, and I'll feel better soon." On the ride to the movies, she threw up and her parents turned the car around and went home. "You always ruin it for everyone!" her sister Kenya yelled at her.

Can you think of a time when you did something to cause a problem for the whole family? What was it?

_____

_____

_____

What was done to correct the situation? Did you work together as a family to work the problem out? How?

_____

_____

_____

Why do you think Kenya was so upset?

_____

_____

_____

How could the problem have been solved?

_____

_____

_____

Aaron is supposed to meet his little sister Kaya after school, but the soccer coach makes him stay late for an extra practice. Kaya waits and waits until he comes, but she's really angry and upset. Aaron tells her to stop being such a baby.

Do you think Kaya is right to be upset? Why or why not?

_____

_____

_____

Do you think Aaron is right to be mad? Why or why not?

_____

_____

_____

Is there anything Aaron could have done to avoid the situation?

_____

_____

_____

Draw a picture of a time when you were afraid that someone forgot about you.

4. PARENT-TO-PARENT PROBLEMS

Parents sometimes have problems getting along. Most of the time, when parents fight, it has nothing to do with the children, and it is never the children's fault. Kids sometimes think that if they behave really well, and never do anything bad, then their parents won't fight. This is wrong. The two have nothing to do with each other. Kids should remember that parents love them even if they have problems and arguments.

Heidi's mother drinks a lot. When she comes home from work, the first thing she does is pour a drink, and then she refills her glass all evening, until she collapses on the sofa. Lately, Heidi's father has been trying to make her mom stop, but they just end up getting into screaming fights. Heidi feels scared, but she's afraid and embarrassed to talk to anyone about it.

Why do you think Heidi feels scared?

_____

_____

_____

Do you think Heidi should try to help her mom stop drinking? Why or why not?

_____

_____

_____

Do you think that Heidi's mom's problem has anything to do with Heidi? Why or why not?

_____

_____

_____

Can you think of a situation when your mom and dad had a problem?

_____

_____

_____

How did it affect you and your brother(s) and sister(s)?

_____

_____

_____

Did you ever try to tell your parents how you were feeling? Did your parents try to make you and your brother(s) and sister(s) feel better? How?

_____

_____

_____

Draw a picture of what you look like when there is a problem in the family.

Now draw a picture of your family after it has solved a problem. What does your family do to feel "close?"

5. SIBLING RIVALRY

Brothers and sisters argue about many things. Common arguments focus on sharing things like toys, bathrooms (especially if you have a big family), clothes, food, and what to watch on TV. But siblings also fight in order to gain the attention of their parents, or to show brothers and sisters who's the "boss."

Myrna and her sister Ellen both try out for the school play. Myrna gets a leading part, while Ellen is picked for the chorus. Their mom is obviously prouder of Myrna than Ellen, and makes a big fuss over helping Myrna practice her lines. Ellen decides to hide Myrna's script, and doesn't give it back for two days.

Why do you think Ellen did this?

_____

_____

_____

Was she right to do this? Why or why not?

_____

_____

_____

Has anything like this ever happened to you? Tell about how you felt.

_____

_____

_____

Draw yourself in the situation you just described.

Billy and his sister Amy have to share a bathroom. Billy thinks he should get more time because he's older and has to look "better." Amy stands at the door screaming for Billy to get out. Billy ignores her and takes his time.

Do you think Billy's reason is a good one? Why or why not?

_____

_____

_____

What do you argue about most with your brother(s) or sister(s)?

_____

_____

_____

Why do you think you argue about it so much?

_____

_____

_____

How do you feel when you are arguing?

_____

_____

_____

Draw you and your sibling arguing about something.

What could you and your brother(s) or sister(s) do to work out the problem together?

_____

_____

_____

How do your parents feel when you argue with your brother(s) or sister(s)?

_____

_____

_____

What are some other things that you fight about with your sibling? What could you do to work out each problem? In the space below, list the problem in one column and a possible solution in the second column.

PROBLEM	SOLUTION
_____	_____
_____	_____
_____	_____
_____	_____
_____	_____
_____	_____

6. FIGHTING FAIR

All families fight. It's normal and healthy to have conflicts, but it's important to remember to fight fair. Fighting fair teaches that conflict is okay, but aggression and violence are not. Fighting fair attacks problems, not people, and it helps everyone involved find solutions to family problems—together.

Ursula and her brother Louis are having a catch. Louis throws a curve and it heads straight for Ursula's head—and it's coming really fast. It's too late for her to duck. "You're the biggest jerk!" Ursula yells at Louis. "You threw the ball at my face! I hate you!"

Keeping in mind the words, "How can we solve this problem?", rephrase what Ursula said to Louis.

_____

_____

_____

Why do you think Ursula was so mad at Louis? Do you think he did it on purpose?

_____

_____

_____

Draw a picture of two children talking instead of fighting. Draw in things that show what the argument is about.

While Betty was playing with her sister Midge's doll, the doll's head came off and wouldn't snap back on. She didn't tell Midge, but when Midge noticed it the next day, she took Betty's doll and drew a mustache on it with a black marker.

Why did Midge want to get even with Betty? Was it fair for her to do this?

_____

_____

_____

What would have been a way to handle this situation which would demonstrate how to "fight fair?"

_____

_____

_____

Have you ever tried to get even with your brother or sister for something he or she did to you? Describe it below.

_____

_____

_____

7. STICKING UP FOR YOURSELF

Sisters and brothers can be cruel to each other. Name-calling, put-downs, teasing, and insults can come at any moment, when everything seems fine and even fun. People put each other down so that they can feel better about themselves, and to feel more secure. Often, one person doesn't even mean to hurt the other. When you stick up for yourself it doesn't mean that you have to get back at the other person—it means that you are making your needs and wants heard without hurting anyone. It means that you are in control and you are on your own "side."

Paolo decided to let his hair grow long enough to pull it back into a ponytail. His sister Rosa thought he looked stupid. "You look like a girl," she told him. "I'm embarrassed to be seen with you!"

Why do you think Rosa felt that way?

_____

_____

_____

Do you think Paolo was entitled to do what he wanted? Why or why not?

_____

_____

_____

Do you think Rosa had a right to criticize him? Why or why not?

_____

_____

_____

If you were Paolo, how would you stick up for yourself?

_____

_____

_____

Draw Rosa saying something positive to Paolo about his appearance.

8. JEALOUSY

Sometimes family members get jealous of things that another person has. A sister can be jealous of her brother's earned money, but she can also be jealous of the attention their father gives to her brother and not to her. Jealousy often involves both material things and things that can't really be measured, like attention and affection.

Mark idolized his older brother Carl. He thought to himself, "He is so cool. Why can't I be like him?" Carl was captain of the football team and had a really pretty girlfriend. Mark struggled to get passing grades and didn't have many friends.

Is there anything Mark could have done to build his self-esteem instead of comparing himself with Carl? Write a few lines about it.

_____

_____

_____

Is it true that Carl was really "cooler" than Mark? Why or why not?

_____

_____

_____

Have you ever been jealous of anyone? What was the outcome?

_____

_____

_____

9. STEPFAMILIES

One of the most difficult family situations involves the "blending" of families. People who already have children marry and all of a sudden the two families must learn to live together. It can be very difficult to live in the same family with someone whom you might not choose to be your friend, much less your brother or sister.

Owen's mom and dad got divorced two years ago. Things were just beginning to settle down when his mom met Larry, and to make things worse, she fell in love with him and now she says she wants to marry him. Owen thinks Larry's okay, but his son Wally is a real geek. How can he live in the same house with him?

What do you think Owen can do to make the situation better?

_____

_____

_____

Is there anything Owen can do to change the situation? What is it?

_____

_____

_____

Tell about a time when things didn't go the way you wanted them to in your stepfamily, or in a friend's stepfamily.

_____

_____

_____

Draw a picture of Owen and Wally. Are they getting along, or are they still enemies?

Sarah's stepmother wants her to call her "Mom." "You're not my mom!" Sarah screams at her, and slams the door. Sarah is furious. How could this strange woman ever think that she can replace Sarah's real mom?

Do you think Sarah should call her stepmother "Mom?" Why or why not?

_____

_____

_____

Is it right for her stepmother to expect Sarah to call her "Mom?" Why or why not?

_____

_____

_____

How can this situation be worked out?

_____

_____

_____

SECTION II: FAMILY VALUES

People tend to like children who behave well and show respect to their parents and other people. When children are taught family values, such as love and respect, these virtues become part of their character and they are viewed by the world as "good" people.

10. HOUSEHOLD RULES

Most families have "rules" and certain expectations of how to behave. Often these rules are set by parents or the head of the household, but it is also a wise idea to allow children to have input into the making of rules and to participate in the decisions about family matters. People who know the rules and follow them get along better with others in general.

A rule in Tanya's family is that the children must do their homework as soon as they come home from school. Tanya's friends decide to go to the local pizza parlor after school and ask Tanya if she wants to go. Tanya doesn't call her mother, and to make matters worse, comes home late for dinner. Tanya's parents are furious, but they are relieved to see that she's okay. Tanya is grounded for the next two weeks.

What could Tanya have done differently in this situation?

_____

_____

_____

Was the consequence she had to pay worth breaking a household rule?
Why or why not?

_____

_____

_____

What are some of your family's important rules? List some of them below:

_____

_____

_____

What do you think would happen if there were no rules in your family?

_____

_____

_____

Have you ever broken any rules? Tell about a time you broke a rule, and why you broke it.

_____

_____

_____

What consequence did you have to pay for breaking that rule?

_____

_____

_____

Draw yourself breaking that rule.

Maria's mom is very unhappy when she sees the mess Maria has made. "Get all this stuff that's on the floor off the floor!," she tells Maria. After she leaves, Maria puts the mess on her bed, making sure that everything is off the floor. Again, her mom has a fit, and punishes her for being a "smart mouth." "But you told me to get everything off the floor!" Maria tells her.

What do you think of Maria's behavior?

_____

_____

_____

Why do you think Maria's mom was so angry each time?

_____

_____

_____

How could Maria's mom have told Maria what she wanted her to do in a better way?

_____

_____

_____

Draw the mess in Maria's room. How do you think it looks?

11. LEARNING RESPONSIBILITY

Parents often expect their children to perform certain duties and chores in order to help in the daily running of the household. Children who are not expected to "pitch in" are not learning the necessary responsibilities that go beyond family life into their real world and they are not becoming sensitive to the needs of others.

Judy's job is putting out the trash. She hates to do it, and she knows that if she doesn't put the trash out, her mom will do it.

JOB CHART

	S	M	T	W	Th	F	S
Trash							
Clean room							
Walk dog							
Make bed							
Feed dog							
Other _____							

What is wrong with the way Judy is thinking?

_____

_____

_____

Do you think her mom should be "harder" on her? Why or why not?

_____

_____

_____

Draw Judy doing something to help her mom.

Do you have certain duties and chores that you are responsible for doing at your house? List a few of your responsibilities.

_____

_____

_____

Sabrina automatically gets allowance every week, even if she doesn't do all her chores. She decides to pay her little sister Lia to make her bed for her every day.

What do you think is wrong with this idea?

_____

_____

_____

Do you think Lia would be making the right decision if she refused to do it?
Why or why not?

_____

_____

_____

12. RESPECTING FELLOW FAMILY MEMBERS

Have you ever heard the expression, "Respect your elders?" It's an even better idea to respect everyone in your family, including those who are your age or even younger than you.

Barry's grandfather tells him that he must eat everything on his dinner plate. Barry hates peas, but even though he never has to eat them at home, he eats them at his grandparent's house.

Why do you think he ate the peas and didn't argue with his grandfather?

_____

_____

_____

Tell how he was respecting his grandfather by eating his peas.

_____

_____

_____

Tell about a time when you showed respect for someone in your family.

_____

_____

_____

Abby borrows her mother's sunglasses. When she gets home, she discovers that the glasses are not in their case. "Mom is going to be really angry," she thinks to herself. "She is always telling me to respect the property of others, and now look what I've done."

What is a "rule" that you should always follow when you borrow something from someone in your family?

_____

_____

_____

What could Abby have done to avoid this problem?

_____

_____

_____

What can Abby do to make things better with her mom?

_____

_____

_____

13. DISCIPLINE IS IMPORTANT

Discipline in a child's life is important because it helps him or her learn that not only will certain behaviors not be tolerated within the family, they also will not be tolerated in society as a whole. When children are exposed to predictable discipline at home, they know the limits and respond accordingly. They also learn to be responsible for their actions.

Bob's mom left extra change all over the house. He found that whenever he took money from her purse, she never noticed. He began to steal money from his friends. "Hey, I'm good at this!" he thought to himself. Soon, he was taking small things from stores, and by then he couldn't stop himself. Finally, he was caught by a security guard. His mother said, "How could this have happened? We never taught you to be a thief!"

How do you think this happened to Bob?

_____

_____

_____

If his mom had disciplined him, do you think it would have happened? Why or why not?

_____

_____

_____

Draw a picture of something Bob could do to make things better.

When Robin goes with her family to her brother's play, she yells to her friends in the audience and carries on with them during the play. Her parents tell her that if she can't be quiet, she has to leave. Finally, they tell her to wait in the lobby for them. They are really angry.

Do you think Robin's parents were being fair? Why or why not?

_____

_____

_____

Why do you think Robin was acting that way?

_____

_____

_____

Draw yourself watching a play.

14. FAMILY LOVE

Love can't be measured or calculated, but it can be given, received, and felt. When you feel love for someone in your family, it's different from the way you might feel about a friend, or other people in your life. Love between family members grows from the bonds they form from growing up together and sharing experiences. It paves the way for healthy relationships outside the family.

Perry's dad always pays more attention to his sister Helen than he does to Perry. When Perry asks for help with his homework, his dad says, "I'm helping Helen now. I'll help you later, okay?" Perry feels that his dad loves Helen more.

Why do you think Perry feels this way?

_____

_____

_____

Do you think it's true? Why or why not?

_____

_____

_____

Draw a picture of Perry dealing with this situation. Is he just coping, or is he solving the problem?

Ricky's mom got divorced and then married her boyfriend Tom. Ricky's mom and Tom did everything together, and never included Ricky. Ricky felt that his mom didn't love him anymore. After all, she got rid of his dad, so why would she want Ricky?

Do you think Ricky's mom really didn't love him anymore?

_____

_____

_____

What could Ricky say to his mom to tell her how he is feeling?

_____

_____

_____

Did anything like this ever happen to you? What was it? How did you feel?

_____

_____

_____

15. TRUST IN THE FAMILY

When you trust someone, you believe that he or she will do something that shows he or she is being responsible. When your parents trust you to do something, it gives them a good feeling because they believe you are mature enough to do it well. If you don't follow through, they will be disappointed, and hopefully, you will learn from that experience so that they will trust you again in the future.

Jeff's dad trusted him to go to school every day. Jeff would leave the house to go to the bus stop in the morning, but sometimes he wouldn't go to school. "They'll never find out," he thought to himself. After a few weeks, however, Jeff's parents got a note from the principal concerning Jeff's absences. "We trusted you to go to school, and now you've really disappointed us, Jeff," his parents said.

Why were Jeff's parents disappointed?

_____

_____

_____

What would you do in this situation if you were Jeff?

_____

_____

_____

Draw Jeff doing the right thing concerning school.

Vicki's mom wanted to go on a date with her boyfriend, but she couldn't find a baby-sitter. She decided that Vicki was old enough to sit for her younger brother and sister. "I am so proud that you are mature enough for me to be able to trust you," her mom says to her.

How do you think this makes Vicki feel?

_____

_____

_____

Do you think Vicki feels excited or nervous or both? Why or why not?

_____

_____

_____

How would you feel if your mom wanted you to baby-sit for your younger siblings?

_____

_____

_____

Draw Vicki baby-sitting for her brother and sister.

16. SELF-ESTEEM AND THE FAMILY

It's often tempting for older siblings to put down their younger brothers and sisters. They do it because it makes them feel powerful. When someone in your family does this, it's helpful to remember that they are probably feeling insecure. That may seem like it's your problem, but it really isn't. You should remember that you can do what you want to do (as long as nobody gets hurt in the process), and no matter how much someone puts you down for it, you should keep on trying anyway. That's part of what self-esteem is—the feeling that you can succeed at doing whatever you want to do.

Zach and his older brother Justin race to the bus stop every morning. Justin always beats Zach, and brags about it to everyone. One morning, Zach beats Justin, and feels really great.

Why do you think it's so important to Justin to beat Zach to the bus stop?

_____

_____

_____

Why do you think Zach felt so great when he beat Justin?

_____

_____

_____

What is something that you could do with your brother or sister that would make you both feel good?

_____

_____

_____

17. FAMILY VALUES ARE UNIVERSAL

Values involve things that are important to you or to others in your family. The positive values you learn through your family can be used as lifelong lessons wherever you go. They can help you be successful in all aspects of your life, and they can help you when things don't seem to be the way you'd like them to be.

Jessica begged her mom to get her a dog for her birthday. She thought her mom had forgotten, but on the morning of her birthday she heard something scratching at her bedroom door. When she opened it, there was the cutest puppy she had ever seen. When she hugged her mom to thank her, her mom said, "I'm so glad you're happy, but I hope you'll take the responsibility of caring for the dog seriously."

With Jessica's example in mind, what is something that you've learned at home about being responsible?

_____

_____

_____

What is a value that you've learned at home that you could use at school?

_____

_____

_____

What is a value that you've learned at home that you could use at the playground?

_____

_____

_____

What is one of the most important values that your parents have taught you?

_____

_____

_____

Draw yourself demonstrating an important value that you have learned from your parents.

18. QUALITY FAMILY TIME

Kenny, Darryl, and Anne's parents take them to the beach every summer. It is something the family has done together for years. It's a chance for everyone to have a good time together after the school year is over. They have a wonderful family vacation. During the school year they also make time for the family to do things together. They go to the movies, go bowling, they go sledding in the snow—they do as many things as a family as time allows.

What are some things that your family does together?

_____

_____

_____

What is your favorite thing to do with your family?

_____

_____

_____

Do you think it is important for family members to participate in activities together? Why or why not?

_____

_____

_____

How would you feel if your family did not do anything together? Why would you feel that way?

_____

_____

_____

Name three new things your family could do together that won't cost any money and would not take much time.

_____

_____

_____

Draw a picture below of your family doing a fun activity together.

SECTION III: FAMILY PROBLEMS

Every family has its problems and conflicts. But conflict can be a good thing, as long as it's dealt with constructively. It can help family members learn new and better ways to respond to problems, build better relationships, and learn more about each other. Problems and conflicts make families look at their differences—together.

19. DEALING WITH DIVORCE

Divorce, especially if it is accompanied by a lot of conflict and bitterness, can lead to continuing problems. Things don't seem the same, because they aren't—but they usually resolve themselves to a point where a family can begin to function again, even though it may be very different.

Barbara's mom and dad have been divorced for six months, but her dad is still depressed about it. Barbara feels bad too, but when she tries to talk to her dad about it, he tells her that it's better if they don't talk about it.

Do you agree with Barbara's dad? Do you think that bad situations will just "go away" if you don't talk about them? Why or why not?

_____

_____

_____

Why do you think it's so hard for Barbara's dad to talk about the divorce with her?

_____

_____

_____

Why do you think Barbara wants to talk with her dad?

_____

_____

_____

Draw a picture of you and a family member having a heart-to-heart conversation.

Vera thinks that if she's very good her parents will decide not to get divorced. She makes her bed, cleans her room, sets the table, and does anything she's asked to do without complaining. Still, her parents announce to her that they are separating.

Why do you think Vera thinks that if she's "good" she can prevent the divorce?

_____

_____

_____

Do you think she's right? Why or why not?

_____

_____

_____

Do you think Vera's parents should consider her feelings before they make their decision? Why or why not?

_____

_____

_____

Have you ever tried to prevent your parents from doing something by behaving in a certain way? What did you do? Did it help?

_____

_____

_____

20. LIVING IN TWO PLACES

If your parents get divorced and you have to live with your mom and with your dad in two different places, it can seem as though your whole world is upside down. But strange and disrupting as this new life may seem, it can offer new experiences and challenges, so that eventually, both places feel like "home."

When Peter left his mom's house to spend the weekend at his dad's, he forgot to take his science book and couldn't study for his test. His dad was angry at him for not being better prepared, and his mom was angry at his dad for not making sure that Peter had what he needed before they left.

Do you think it was right for Peter's dad to be angry? Why or why not?

_____

_____

_____

Do you think it was right for Peter's mom to be angry? Why or why not?

_____

_____

_____

What could Peter do so that he doesn't forget important things when he goes from one place to the other?

_____

_____

_____

Draw something that could help you remember important things.

Whenever Susan came home from a weekend with her mom, her dad would ask her a lot of questions about things she didn't feel like talking about. He'd ask, "Who is Mom going out with now?" and "Does Mom ever talk about me?" He would also tell her to look through her mom's mail to see if there was anything from people her dad didn't know. Her mom would threaten her and say, "If you tell Dad anything I'll punish you."

Was it fair to put Susan in the middle? Why or why not?

_____

_____

_____

Do you think her parents were deliberately being unfair to her?

_____

_____

_____

What would be something constructive that Susan could say to her parents?

_____

_____

_____

Have you ever been put in a situation like this? Were you caught in the middle of your parents' problems? Describe it, and tell how you felt.

_____

_____

_____

21. DIFFERENT KINDS OF FAMILIES

The world is made up of all kinds of families. Some have two parents, some have one. Some children live with their grandparents or other relatives. Some live with foster parents. None of these are better than others: they're just different.

Kara lived with her grandparents because her parents had been killed in a car accident. She had lived with them since she was a baby, so she didn't think much about it until she began to see that other kids had parents who were younger. Her friends began to tease her about it, and she began to feel embarrassed.

Why do you think Kara felt embarrassed?

_____

_____

_____

Why do you think her friends teased her?

_____

_____

_____

Do you know any families that do not have two parents? Write about them.

_____

_____

_____

Owen was jealous of Joe because Joe's parents seemed happy together and Joe's family always did things together. Owen's mom worked two jobs and she was rarely home, and when she was, she was too busy to pay much attention to him or his brother.

Why was Owen jealous of Joe?

_____

_____

_____

What could he do to feel better?

_____

_____

_____

What could Owen do to change his own family situation?

_____

_____

_____

Draw your family below, and name three things that are good about it.

22. STEPSIBLINGS

When people who have children from a previous marriage get married, often these children have to live together as a "family." Under the best circumstances, it's hard to live with people you hardly know and may not even like very much. Everyone has to do his or her best to get along.

Ira hated having to move into his stepmother's house. It was smaller than his dad's house, and he had to share a room with his stepbrother Joel. He didn't even like Joel—he was two years younger and a real geek! When he tried to talk to his dad about it, all his dad could say was, "It's the best we can do for now. You'll have to make the best of it."

Why do you think Ira's dad said that?

_____

_____

_____

What do you think "making the best of it" would mean?

_____

_____

_____

What could Ira do to get to know Joel?

_____

_____

_____

Draw Ira and Joel in their room.

Perry and Lance were really good friends at school, but when their parents started to date each other and finally announced that they were getting married, things between them got kind of weird. They both felt funny around each other, especially when they realized that they were going to be stepbrothers and they would be living together.

Why do you think they felt that way?

_____

_____

_____

How would you feel if you found out that your good friend was going to be your stepbrother or stepsister? Why?

_____

_____

_____

What would you say to Perry and Lance to make the situation easier to talk about?

_____

_____

_____

23. RELIGIOUS ISSUES

The world is made up of all kinds of families who are of many different religions. Some families believe in one God, others believe in many, and still others don't observe any religion at all. It's their personal privilege to do whatever feels right to them.

Saul lives next to Sam, whose family strictly observes the dietary laws of Judaism. This means that Sam can't eat at Saul's house. When he invites Sam and is turned down, Saul thinks Sam is being a snob.

What do you think? What should Sam tell Saul?

_____

_____

_____

Can the two boys still be friends? Why or why not?

_____

_____

_____

What do you think about people observing their own religions? Do you think a person's religion "matters?"

_____

_____

_____

Have you ever visited a house of worship of a faith other than yours? Draw a picture of your experience.

24. MONEY PROBLEMS

It's hard to be the only kid at school who doesn't have something, like a certain kind of sneakers, or the right clothes, or the latest kind of book bag. It's embarrassing when your parents can't afford to buy you things you really want. Some kids earn money to pay for such things, others have to do without them.

Marty's mom just lost her job, and his dad has been out of work for weeks. He knows he'll never have the money to buy that boom box he's had his eye on, much less the tapes he wants to play in it. He arranges to swap some earrings he finds in his mom's drawer for a "used" boom box. When his parents ask him where he got the boom box, he says a friend gave it to him.

Why do you think Marty didn't ask his parents for the money for the boom box?

_____

_____

_____

The swap didn't involve any money. Do you think he was right to make the swap? Why or why not?

_____

_____

_____

What would you do if you wanted something really badly but didn't have the money to buy it?

_____

_____

_____

Pamela has to work after school to help her parents pay the rent. All of her sisters and brothers have had to do this since they were old enough to get a job. "We can't afford to support all of you," they tell the children. "This will help you learn to be responsible."

Do you think it's fair for parents to expect children to pay "rent?" Why or why not?

_____

_____

_____

What would you do if your parents told you to get a job so that you could help buy food or pay the rent?

_____

_____

_____

Draw Pamela at her job. What do you think it would be?

25. APPEARANCE CAN MAKE A LASTING IMPRESSION

Appearance can be really important because people often form their first impressions of you from how you look, not from who you are. Once they get past the first impression, they usually decide whether or not they want to get to know you. Kids often want to "look" like everyone else. But parents sometimes don't understand this.

Amanda's mother insisted that she wear her sister's hand-me-downs. "They fit you perfectly, and they're not worn out at all!" she says. Amanda is humiliated—she doesn't want to wear old clothes. She wants to wear what everyone else is wearing!

What do you think Amanda should do?

_____

_____

_____

Why do you think it's so important for kids to be like "everyone else?"

_____

_____

_____

Has anything like this ever happened to you? Tell about it.

_____

_____

_____

Draw Amanda in the clothes she has to wear, and in the clothes she wants to wear.

26. DRUGS AND ALCOHOL

Parents will almost always tell you to stay away from kids who use drugs, drink, or smoke cigarettes, but sometimes it's hard to resist. It's important to remember that you can get into trouble through the company you keep, even if you don't smoke or drink. It's just as easy to find friends who have other interests as friends who drink or get high.

Vince's parents smoke cigarettes. They say that it's a bad habit and they want to quit, and that they don't want Vince to smoke or drink.

Do you think Vince's parents are right? Why or why not?

_____

_____

_____

What would you think if you were Vince?

_____

_____

_____

Mary's mom has asked her to be a "spy" for her. She wants her to report anything her sister Kate does that's wrong. Mary walks in on Kate just as Kate and her friends are about to share a six-pack of beer. Kate warns Mary, "If you tell Mom I'll never trust you again."

What do you think Mary should do? Why?

_____

_____

_____

Have you ever been told by a sibling to keep a secret? What happened?

_____

_____

_____

How do you feel about a parent asking a child to be a "spy?"

_____

_____

_____

Draw Mary making her decision.

27. SCHOOL PERFORMANCE

Problems at home can affect a person's grades and overall performance at school. Sometimes children have problems at school that are the result of problems at home. For example, a kid whose mother is very ill may be really upset, and this could cause him to daydream in class and forget to do his homework. Or a child whose parents fight all the time may be really angry, and he may decide not to do his schoolwork as a way to get back at them.

Chris was a good student. He studied a lot and got As and Bs on his tests and papers. But in the middle of the year, he began to hang out with kids who didn't like school and he started staying out late and missing classes. His grades went down and his parents didn't know what to do.

What would you do if you were Chris's parents?

_____

_____

_____

What would you say to Chris?

_____

_____

_____

What would you do if your friends didn't care about school or grades?

_____

_____

_____

Amy has a decision to make. She was picked to be on the cheerleading team, but this requires that she stay after school every day for practice. Her grades aren't very good, and her parents aren't happy about her being on the team. They tell her that her grades have to come up before she can be on the team.

What do you think Amy should do?

_____

_____

_____

How would you handle this situation?

_____

_____

_____

Have you ever had to study harder in order to maintain your grades when you had extracurricular activities? Write about it.

_____

_____

_____

Draw Amy on the cheerleading team.

SECTION IV: THE FUTURE

Do you ever wonder what your life will be like when you're all grown up? Most kids have some idea of what they want to be when they grow up. Will you get married and have children like your parents? What will your children be like, look like, and act like? What kind of parent will you be? Will you have a job and a career?

In the space below, draw a picture of yourself all grown-up. What do you look like? Do you wear special clothes for your job? Do you have a wife or husband? Do you have any children? Pets? What does your family look like? However you see yourself in the future is how you should draw your picture.

28. YOU AND YOUR FUTURE FAMILY

It's fun to think of yourself with a family in the future. Here's a chance to look into the future and do things according to how you, as a kid, think they should be done as an adult.

Leon is in college. He lives at home, and commutes to school every day. He thinks his parents should stay out of his business, and just let him come and go as he pleases. They say that since he still lives at home, they have a right to tell him what to do.

What do you think? Do you agree with Leon or with his parents?

_____

_____

_____

What would you say to a teenager who told you that he or she was old enough to make his or her own decisions?

_____

_____

_____

Faye has a really good relationship with her parents. She likes spending time with them, even though she has her own apartment and car and job. She invites some friends to join her and her parents for dinner one night. One of them says, "Why do you spend so much time with your parents? You're a big girl now—why do you need them all the time?"

If you were Faye, would your feelings be hurt? Why or why not?

_____

_____

_____

What would you say if you were Faye?

_____

_____

_____

Do you think you could have a relationship with your parent(s) like Faye has with hers? Why or why not?

_____

_____

_____

As a parent, what kind of relationship do you think you will have with your children?

_____

_____

_____

Draw yourself as a parent.

29. YOU MAKE THE RULES

Do your parents make the rules in your family? Do you help them decide what the rules should be? Here's a chance for you to decide how this process should take its course.

RULES CHART

1. Rooms must be neat.
2. Beds must be made.
3. No TV before homework is done.
4. No name-calling or put downs.
5. Everyone is entitled to his or her opinion.

Sarah's parents made a rule that homework had to be done before any of the children could go outside and play or watch TV. The kids in the neighborhood decided to have a marathon kickball game right after school. When Sarah asked her parents if she could do her homework after the game, they said, "A rule's a rule. You have to do your homework before you can play."

Do you agree with Sarah's parents? Why or why not?

_____

_____

_____

What would you do if you were Sarah's parents in this situation?

_____

_____

_____

Do you think it's a bad or good thing to make an exception sometimes? Why?

_____

_____

_____

What are two rules in your family that you feel could be broken as exceptions (just one time)?
Explain what would happen if they were broken.

_____

_____

_____

Cesar knew that he was not allowed to take money from his mother's purse, but he needed a dollar to buy something form the ice cream truck, and she wasn't home. He found a five dollar bill and took it. After he bought the ice cream, he decided to keep the extra money.

What do you think of what Cesar did?

_____

_____

_____

Do you think he was right to take the money? After all, his mother wasn't home, and if she had been, he would have asked her.

_____

_____

_____

Imagine yourself as a parent. What would you do if your child broke a rule? How would you handle it?

_____

_____

_____

Draw yourself handling the situation when your child breaks a rule.

30. SIDING WITH ONE CHILD

It's often hard for a parent to decide which child has started a fight, and which child should suffer the consequences. Some parents punish both children. Others decide on the spur of the moment who is the guilty one. Let's see what you would do.

William's brother Sandy threw a ball at his head. William stood up quickly and knocked his glass over, spilling chocolate milk all over the living room rug. William's parents sent him to his room without even scolding Sandy, even when he said it was Sandy's fault.

Why do you think William's parents thought it was his fault?

_____

_____

_____

Was it his fault? Was what William did worse than what Sandy did to him?

_____

_____

_____

If you were their parents, how would you handle the situation?

_____

_____

_____

What would you say to your children if they were fighting with each other?

_____

_____

_____

Do you think it's normal for siblings to fight? Why or why not?

_____

_____

_____

Debra is physically disabled and must be in a wheelchair. She can do many things by herself, but she needs others to help her with certain things. Her brother Pete is getting really tired of having to do everything for her, and he also feels neglected because no one ever pays attention to him.

Why do you think Pete feels this way?

_____

_____

_____

What do you think he should do about his feelings?

_____

_____

_____

What would you do if your son or daughter had a handicap?

_____

_____

_____

Draw yourself with your child.

31. ANGER CAN HURT

Try to put yourself in the parent's position when you answer the following questions.

Byron's parents both worked until 8 p.m. every day. Byron and his brothers had to fend for themselves after school, for dinner, and through homework time. When Byron got a part in the school play, his parents were happy for him, but neither one could come to see the play. He said, "That's okay. Why should you come to my play? You never spend any time with me anyway. You don't care about me at all."

How do you think Byron felt when he said this? Why did he feel that way?

_____

_____

_____

What do you think his parents could do to make things better?

_____

_____

_____

What would you say to your child in a situation like this?

_____

_____

_____

Norman's mom came home from work in a bad mood. Norman had been waiting for her for hours, because he needed help with his homework. When he asked for her help, she screamed, "I can't help you now! Why can't you see that I've had a terrible day?"

How could Norman have "seen" that his mom had a bad day?

_____

_____

_____

Do you think his mom was being fair? Why or why not?

_____

_____

_____

How would you act towards your family if you had a bad day at work and wanted to be left alone? How would you let them know that you were feeling badly?

_____

_____

_____

Draw Norman and his mom talking it out.

32. A DAY IN THE LIFE OF YOUR FAMILY

What is it like at your house on a typical day? Perhaps your family always does the same things on weekdays and weekends. This is called having a "routine," where everyone knows what is expected of them, and most of the time, they do it. Some families go about their business as individuals, sometimes coming together for meals or activities.

In Brenda's family, everyone is always coming or going in a rush. Her parents work, her brother's on the football team and has practice every day, her sister baby-sits often, and she is in the French Club that meets after school. Everyone is self-sufficient, but the entire family knows that once a week, on Friday night, everyone is expected to be home at 5 p.m. to help prepare and enjoy dinner together.

Do you think eating together is an important activity for a family? Why or why not?

_____

_____

_____

Do you think Brenda's family is "too busy?" Why or why not?

_____

_____

_____

List some of the things that you would like to happen in a day with your future family.

Morning:

_____

_____

_____

Afternoon:

_____

_____

_____

Evening:

_____

_____

_____

What activities (reading, playing games, going to ball games, shopping, taking walks, etc.) would you participate in with your children?

_____

_____

_____

What kind of responsibilities (taking care of pets, cleaning their rooms, etc.) would your children have?

_____

_____

_____

What responsibilities would you, as a parent, have?

_____

_____

_____

33. BEING IN A FAMILY IS NOT ALWAYS EASY

Families are made up of all different people who just happen to be related. They have different wants, needs, goals, problems, etc. They also have their own "dreams," as shown below. When you really think about it, it's pretty amazing that family members manage to live together. As a parent, it would be your "job" to deal with all those different things that make your children unique individuals. Here's a chance to think about how you would handle some "sticky" situations.

Jack decided that since his room was his, nobody, including his parents, could tell him what to do with it. So he decided to paint it black, and he never cleaned it. His parents were furious. "You have destroyed our house!" they yelled at Jack. "As long as you live with us, you will do what *we* say!"

Who was right? Why?

_____

_____

_____

What would have been a better way to handle the situation?

_____

_____

_____

Should Jack have done anything before he made this decision? Tell what you think.

_____

_____

_____

What would you do if your child did something like this?

_____

_____

_____

Franco's friend Tim wanted him to help him with a drug deal he was going to make. Franco knew he shouldn't, and after he thought a lot about it, he decided to ask his parents for their advice on how to say "no" to Tim.

Do you think this was wise? Why or why not?

_____

_____

_____

How do you think Franco's parents felt when he came to them for help?

_____

_____

_____

Would you want your children to come to you for advice and help? Why or why not?

_____

_____

_____

How do you think you would feel if your child asked for your help?

_____

_____

_____

Tell about three values that your parents have taught you that you could pass on to your children.

_____

_____

_____

Would you say that the lessons you have learned from your parents will help you be a "better" parent with your own children? Explain your answer.

_____

_____

_____

Draw your future family dealing with a problem together.

After completing all the exercises in this workbook, share your answers with your family. Just by doing this you are bringing everyone together to participate in an activity. Maybe you will be able to change some things in your family that aren't so great. Maybe you will make some things that are good even better!